# cat massage

# cat massage

## expert know-how at your fingertips

Nicola Routledge

illustrations by Bo Lundberg

MQP

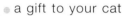

# introduction

There's nothing more satisfying than having a cat on your lap, purring loudly with complete contentment. Whether you're the proud owner of a mischievous moggie or a sleek, pedigree princess, learning to use the gentle art of cat massage will have your favorite feline in seventh heaven. Cats are delightfully sensuous creatures, and frequently invite you to caress and pet them. Now, with this enchanting little book, you'll be able to express your love with real knowledge at your fingertips.

Massage is a wonderful way of caring for your cat. It calms nerves, reduces fear, soothes aches and pains, improves muscle tone, promotes a gleaming, healthy coat, and creates an extra-special bond between you both. What's more, it's good for your health too—massaging your cat is a great way of getting relaxed, and can even lower your blood pressure. With detailed, practical, exercises and techniques on how to massage every area of your cat's body, from ears to paws, from tail to tummy, your pet will soon be glowing with health and well-being.

The witty, affectionate, and oh-so-knowing illustrations by the well-known Swedish artist Bo Lundberg capture every nuance of feline response— they are utterly endearing and will steal your heart as well!

A little note to the reader *In order to avoid constant repetition of the phrase "he or she" in the text, we have referred to the cat as "she" throughout* Cat Massage. *So, if you own a male cat, be assured that this is entirely arbitrary, and that your pet will benefit from being massaged in equal measure.*

# 1    a gift to your cat

# sheer heaven!

Have you ever enjoyed a deep, satisfying, and relaxing massage? If so, you already appreciate how wonderful it feels. However, you may not have given much thought to massaging your kitty. Think about it—you'll realize that massage is one of the greatest gifts you can give your favorite feline. It should become an integral part of her regular care.

Cats are delightfully sensuous creatures. They frequently invite you to caress and pet them, and who can resist such a delightful invitation? Of course, it's not only your cat who enjoys the experience; stroking your feline friend is highly pleasurable for you as well. Actually, this casual act is just an everyday variant of massage, so you don't need to feel that it's all too complicated for you to learn. The skills described here are a more developed form of ordinary petting. The rewards are tangible, though, and can be truly dramatic. Soon you'll see and feel positive changes in your cat's overall health and behavior.

*Your cat gets an immense amount of pleasure from simply rubbing her face against your leg—so think how much more she'll get from a skillful massage.*

Massage has many functions—it is a powerful communicative method, a healing art, and an excellent form of preventative healthcare. You don't have to attend special classes and it doesn't cost you anything to learn how to do it. All you have to do is devote a little time to learning some basic skills. You may feel a little timid or inadequate about becoming a cat masseur. But don't worry! These massage techniques are very simple, and your cat will thank you for learning them.

# mutual satisfaction

You may think that your cat is happy enough without massage, but she is missing out from the positive benefits to be gained from it. This is even more crucial in a world of hectic schedules, where most people are at work all day and their cats spend long periods alone. If this is the case for you and your cat, regular massage will not only improve her health, it will also give her quality time, affection, and attention. Once you've become proficient, you may want to teach the rest of your family how to massage her. It's a great feeling to know that you can all help make a positive difference in your cat's enjoyment of life.

Massage is a highly focused way of touching, and if you've ever enjoyed one yourself, you'll certainly know the good physical and emotional feelings that you experience during a session. It is just the same for your cat and you will notice differences in her soon afterward. A massage boosts her physical well-being by relaxing her muscles and soothing her aches and pains. From the psychological point of view, the effect is both relaxing and comforting and helps build a firm bond between the two of you.

# for those difficult moments

**Tense, nervous** If your cat is a nervous jumpy, character, regular massage will calm and reassure her and make her feel more secure. Highly strung cats gradually become more relaxed and stop overreacting when approached, when being groomed, or when picked up. Longhaired cats are often especially hard to groom—many simply hate it, but after they've enjoyed a massage, they will relax.

**Going to the vet** Cats seem to have a sixth sense about when they are due to visit the vet. Some put up a violent struggle. Massage will help in such cases. It teaches your cat to enjoy being handled and makes veterinary visits less frightening—and easier on you and the vet!

**Other people** It is very helpful if you can figure out the massage strokes she likes best—your cat will let you know what they are. You can then invite friends and relatives to massage her using those particular strokes. She will then become increasingly confident, relaxed, and happy to be handled by different people.

*A visit to the vet can turn into a major battle, but
regular massage will calm your cat's nerves.*

# a healthy routine

Massage has a direct effect on your cat's health because it increases the blood supply to the muscles by improving circulation. This is very important because blood moves nutrients and oxygen throughout the body and also helps to remove waste products. This is beneficial for cats of all ages. For older cats, massage can ease their aches and pains, while a "fingertip" massage for kittens at the end of a hard day's fun and games helps strengthen and tone their muscles.

It is also an excellent early warning system for possible health problems. Changes in your cat's physical condition are often detectable before you can see them. You are more likely to discover unusual growths, skin and hair conditions, and infestations of ticks or lice if you are giving her regular massages. This also gives you the opportunity to discuss your concerns with the vet at the onset of any problem.

# first class results

If you are the proud owner of a show-cat, you'll find that massage promotes a gleaming coat and muscle tone. Your cat will also learn to relax when the judges are handling her. Massage will make a real improvement in your cat's mood and temperament at the shows.

*What a star! Massage can help your cat win prizes for her glowing health, relaxed deportment, and calm temperament.*

# good for you too

You probably have an instinctive belief that being touched is good for your health, without knowing exactly why. However, scientists undertook important work on this subject as far back as the 1950s. It was then that a research project at the University of Wisconsin first demonstrated that the experience of being touched was vital for all aspects of animal well-being. The study showed that young animals who were taken away from a litter at birth developed physical, behavioral, and medical problems even though they were well-nourished. The conclusion was that both animals and humans need regular physical contact to thrive and feel completely happy

Massage is not only immensely soothing to your cat, it is also a real boost to your own health. Research has proven that the responses of elderly folks, invalids, and people recovering from surgery to stroking animals include lowered blood pressure, increased peace of mind, and a greater sense of happiness.

A regular massage will also improve the quiet communication and bond between you and your cat. She will very much appreciate this special, skillful attention, and you will gain greater insight into her personality. What better reward could you ask for than the pleasure, comfort, and sense of peace derived from your massage sessions?

*Giving your cat regular massage sessions reduces stress for you both, and helps to creates a loving, trusting bond between you.*

# 2 getting to know your cat

# cat in action

You don't need a degree in anatomy to understand the basics of how your cat's body works. Although massage concentrates primarily on the muscles, being aware of the whole system helps you understand why your cat needs massage. This enables you to do a better job and helps you to more accurately monitor your cat's responses.

Your cat is able to move around thanks to her superb locomotory and nervous systems.

The locomotory system includes:

• **bones** (skeletal system)

• **muscles** (muscular system)

• **tendons and ligaments**

**The skeletal system** includes approximately 250 bones—the longer the cat's tail is, the more bones there are in it. Bones create a solid framework, giving your cat her distinct form, protecting her soft internal organs, and providing levers that she uses to move her body from one place to another. Her vertebrae are less tightly connected than yours; that's why her spine is so much more flexible and why she can arch into a U-shape or twist and turn to squeeze through the tiniest gaps.

*Your cat is amazingly flexible and can arch
her body to slink through the smallest spaces.*

# poetry in motion

Cat lovers are enthralled at the sheer beauty and grace exhibited by a feline moving around in her natural element. The range and power of these movements are amazing—one moment she's curled up and seemingly asleep, the next leaping effortlessly onto a wall to observe a tiny insect that she has somehow glimpsed.

Your cat uses her locomotory system every day to fulfill all her basic needs, such as hunting, feeding, and marking her territory. In a healthy cat, this system becomes strengthened and remains resilient through a combination of daily use and daily rest. If your cat uses a lot of energy, her locomotory system needs adequate time and rest so that her body can make its own repairs. This natural repair process is fundamental to your cat's strength and fitness. Older cats take longer to recover from activity, and kittens must build up their strength as they grow.

Regular massage is a valuable aid in this essential repair process. It increases the blood supply to the muscles and surrounding tissues, improves the efficiency of waste removal from the tissues, and improves the influx of oxygen and nutrients into the body.

# massage and the nervous system

The nervous system communicates with the locomotory system like a telephone switchboard. Nerves run all through the body, often crossing, and send messages by way of electrical impulses. Messages constantly go to the brain and from there, the brain continually sends them out to your cat's body, even during sleep.

Massage is known to improve nerve stimulation and, therefore, helps to increase your cat's control of her locomotory system. This is particularly important for cats who have difficulty moving. Older cats, or those suffering from an accident or injury, benefit greatly from regular massage sessions. In time, your cat will feel less pain and move more freely. If your cat has areas of her body that are lacking sensation for any reason, regular massage will increase the nerve function.

There are also psychological benefits to massage—stimulating the muscles and skin of your cat promotes relaxation and a calm attitude. Massage promotes relaxation and therefore increases trust between the two of you. Don't forget that massage is also a valuable *desensitization* technique. It calms cats that are "hyper-sensitive" to touch, particularly when being groomed. It helps eliminate mild aches and pains by removing toxins so that sore muscles can heal.

# healthy,supple muscles

Massage works directly on your cat's muscles, so it helps to know where these are and what they do. Some are situated deep in the body, others near the skin's surface—so you'll need to use different strokes according to which muscle is being treated.

**The muscular system** includes all the muscles in your cat's body, large and small. Some are used to maintain a stance for long periods without tiring—for example, when she is crouched to stalk prey. Others are used for fast movements such as pouncing, chasing, and playing.

**The tendons and ligaments** These complete the locomotory system. The tendons link the muscles to the bones and the ligaments bind bones to other bones.

# feline muscles

### Head and face muscles
Functions—chewing, biting, licking, swallowing, facial expressions
*Masseter, Buccinator, Temporal*

### Neck muscles
Functions—turning, rotating, craning
*Trapezius, Latissimus dorsi, Brachiocephalicus*

### Ear muscles
Functions—moves the ears back and up
*Auricular*

### Shoulder and foreleg muscles
Functions—walking, running, stretching, scratching
*Biceps, Deltoid, Latissimus dorsi, Trapezius, Triceps*

### Back muscles
Functions—turning, stretching, raising
*Latissimus dorsi, Trapezius*

### Upper hind leg and rump muscles
Functions—walking, running, jumping, scratching
*Biceps femoris, Gastrocnemius, Gluteals*

## Abdominal muscles

Functions—support the organs
of the abdomen
*External obliques, Rectus abdominus*

## Chest muscles

Functions—connect the ribs, flex
the shoulder
*Intercostals, Pectorals*

## Forepaw muscles

Functions—scratching, washing, digging
*Flexors, Extensors*

## Tail muscles

Functions—moving the tail
Controlled by the muscles of the
lower back

When you are massaging, you will
work on groups of these muscles,
using a variety of strokes and
focusing on specific points for
special therapeutic use.

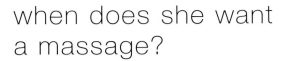

# when does she want a massage?

You can do a massage at any time. But if you settle on a special time each day, you and your cat will look forward to that moment. Pick somewhere relaxing and reasonably quiet: a cozy chair, the living room couch, a bed, or in the garden on a sunny afternoon. Most cats have a favorite spot to relax and that can be a good spot for the massage.

# yes, she's ready

Cats will welcome a massage when they are not busy hunting, feeding, washing, checking out territories, or doing anything else active. Welcoming signs include meowing for attention, purring when you approach or touch her, or half-closing her eyes—a signal of trust in your friendship.

*There's no mistaking a fully relaxed feline. At her most trusting, your cat will roll over and show her tummy. Yes, she'd love a massage!*

# reading her signals

It is important to look for and correctly interpret the signals your cat gives out.
Here are the most common ones that you will encounter:

**Meow, Meow** Wild cats rarely meow, but your domestic cat has to use this sound in order to talk to you. As you will already know, a meow is a powerful communication tool. Your cat will meow for attention, but the sound varies depending on the message. One type of meow means that your cat wants to be let out, another means she wants to be fed, and another could be a demand for a massage. In time, you will become more aware of the different sounds—especially those before, during, and after a massage.

**Chirrup** Your cat may also make a soft chirruping sound. She may make this sound when she is on her way to the food bowl. Other times, it can be an invitation to "come along with me." And your cat may use the same sound to say she wants a massage.

**Purr, purr!** The sound most associated with cats is purring. A purring cat is friendly, submissive, reassured, and contented. Some cats purr in anticipation of the pleasure they associate with massage. Others will purr once massage has begun or after they are fully relaxed.

**Caterwauling** You'll usually hear this aggressive sound at night when two male cats are sizing each other up for a fight. It starts with low-pitched warning tones and can quickly escalate into full-blown screaming as they exchange blows.

*Some cats can be highly vocal and want to "talk" to you all the time. It's important to pay attention to the different sounds so you can understand what they mean.*

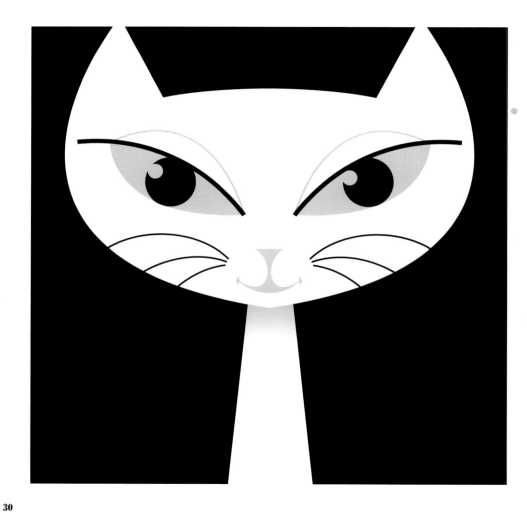

**Watch those eyes** Your cat's eyes will tell you a lot about her thoughts and feelings. They can change from dark slits to open pools of light in a matter of seconds. An alert cat will have fully opened eyes; you'll see this when she senses strangers or is worried. Half-closed eyes demonstrate trust and relaxation—extremely good signs during a massage. Yawning also shows contentment and trust. Wide-open eyes can indicate blissful enjoyment or, conversely, extreme pain or fright. That's why you should continually monitor and assess your cat's responses to your massage.

*If you want to check out your cat's mood, just look into her eyes. Wide open pupils like these may mean that she's either blissfully happy or scared.*

**Ears up?** The positioning of your cat's ears is another sign of what she is thinking. Perked up ears indicate a happy, relaxed cat—one ready to receive a massage. If you touch a sensitive or sore area, a cat may show annoyance by turning back her ears while her whiskers bristle forward—respond by continuing with extra care.

**Tail talk** Much of your cat's communication occurs through her tail—it can be the most expressive part of her body. A tail that curves gently up and down at the tip indicates a relaxed cat, a cat without a care in the world. A tail held high with a soft curve in the middle is a signal of interest—maybe in your approach. A fully erect tail is a no-holds-barred invitation to approach and massage.

**Welcome!** A tail held erect but with the tip tilted over means "welcome"—with some reservations. A cat with her tail between her legs is showing extreme submission. Relax her and build up her confidence with a slow, gentle massage. Don't overdo it. If the cat is not wholeheartedly pleased by the massage, keep it short and get her used to its sensations before extending the time for which you do it.

**Go away!** A tail twitched from side to side at the tip indicates mild irritation, whereas a tail swished vigorously back and forth proclaims anger. If the tail is up and bristled, the cat is feeling aggressive and is not willing to be massaged. An arched and bristled tail is the mark of a cat both defensive and aggressive—e.g., a cat that feels cornered.

**Scared stiff** If the cat is holding her tail low and fluffed out, hold off on the massage. This cat is very frightened. Flattened ears also tell you that your cat is fearful, especially if her pupils are dilated and her whiskers are pulled back.

**Hiss!** Normally, a frightened cat runs and hides; she tried to draw as little attention to herself as possible. However, if she feels cornered, she may yowl, spit, or hiss. Build up a relationship of trust before trying a massage. A cat who is not in the right mood for massage will quickly move away from you. If she is upset, her body will be tense, her eyes wide, and she may hiss.

*A tail bristled up like a bottle brush and ears flattened back are clear signs that your cat is feeling aggressive and is not happy to be massaged.*

*Your cat will simply run for cover and hide if she feels threatened in any way. If she's nervous about having a massage, don't force her—wait until she's ready.*

# when not to massage your cat

Don't massage:

- if your cat appears ill, lethargic, or is not eating
- if she has a high temperature, fast pulse, or is breathing rapidly
- if there is pain, swelling, or heat in any area of her body
- if she has an injury that is less than seven days old
- if she is lame—unless the vet thinks that massage is appropriate

Sometimes your cat doesn't appear to be her usual healthy self, and may have a virus or infection. In that case, massage will not help her; in fact, it could make her feel worse. Massage helps release lactic acid and other toxins that build up in the muscle fibers. When these waste products are released, the blood-stream carries them away to be expelled. When the body is fighting off an infection, releasing muscle toxins slows down the healing process.

When she has a wound, clotting prevents the excessive loss of fluids and starts the healing process. This is also true for a bruise, which is the result of burst blood vessels under the skin. Massage may reinjure a wound or a bruise that is less than seven days old. If you are in doubt about when the injury occurred, wait longer—wait until you are sure that sufficient time has passed for the healing process to be complete. If the injury is localized, you can massage the rest of your cat's body, but be careful and don't get too close to the injured area.

# the new mother

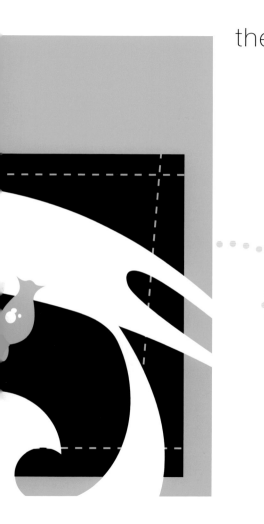

Although many pregnant cats enjoy a massage, you should be especially careful at this time. After she has given birth, wait until the kittens are at least two weeks old to massage her. By then, she will have completely recovered from labor.

*A mother cat has a lot of work to do looking after her litter of new kittens. All she needs is peace, quiet, and privacy. Later on, when her kittens are older, she will appreciate getting back to her regular massage sessions.*

# is your cat healthy?

**If your cat is healthy, she is likely to enjoy a massage.**

A cat in good health shows the following signs:

- "well padded"—that is, she is the right weight and the ratio between her muscle tissue and her body fat is appropriate for her breed. Breeds have a lot of variation: Siamese cats have very prominent skeletal frames, for example, and a barn cat is leaner than the average family pet. Some cats are much bigger and broader—it is far more common to see cats that are overweight than underweight
- alertness—aware and interested in what is going on
- eating and drinking normal amounts
- salmon-pink mucous membranes in the gums and around the eye
- supple and shiny skin and coat
- no abnormal heat spots or swellings on her body or legs.
- body temperature of 101–102.5° F (38.33–39.17° C)—use the thermometer with care!
- steady on her feet—no hopping or limping
- no discharge from the eyes, ears, or nose
- normal feces
- light yellow urine

# is your cat unwell?

**If your cat is sick, have the vet see her before doing massage.**

Do not proceed with your massage if:

- part of the skeletal frame, such as her ribs or backbone, is unusually prominent
- your cat is not completely alert; that is, she is unresponsive or apathetic
- your cat is not eating or drinking normal amounts
- mucous membranes in the mouth or around the eyes are not salmon pink. A pale color indicates anemia or infection; yellow indicates jaundice or liver disease; blue indicates a lack of oxygen or poor blood circulation
- skin and coat are dull and matted
- areas of her body are abnormally hot or swollen
- her feces are not their normal consistency or quantity
- her urine is discolored
- her temperature is abnormal
- she is lame and displays hopping, uneven steps, or stiffness
- she is discharging thick, smelly mucous from her eyes or nose
- her eyes are not fully open or the third eyelid is extended
- her behavior is abnormal
- her weight is excessive

# 3 basic massage strokes

There are three basic strokes: palming, tapping, and compression.

*The palming or effleurage stroke shown here is so easy to learn, and is the one you will use most. With practice, you'll soon get it right—and your cat will love the smooth, gliding, motion.*

# palming

**A long, gentle, stroking movement, this stroke relaxes your cat, stimulates the nerves close to the surface of the skin, and increases blood circulation in the muscles there.**

This is also called *effleurage*. Glide your palms over her body in a smooth movement, with your hands flat. You will develop a sense of how light or heavy a touch to use. Some cats prefer a very gentle touch, others are ticklish and need a firmer pressure. Watch your cat to see if she is enjoying the massage. If she is, her eyes may close, or she may yawn, purr, or relax completely. Some cats push against your hands and increase the pressure of the massage themselves.

Always work in the same direction as her coat lies. Stroke from the neck to the tail and from the shoulders and hind end to the paws. If your cat enjoys it, you can use the tips of your fingers in gentle *effleurage* strokes over her face, under her chin, down her limbs to the paws, and down her tail.

This is the stroke you will use most often. It allows you and your cat to become familiar with massage together and helps you to gauge the spots where your cat enjoys or dislikes being massaged. It also prepares her for the next stage of the massage.

# feel with your fingers

While massaging, pay attention to the way your cat's body feels under your fingers and palms. Is any area hot? or cool? Does she have hot or cold spots on both sides of her body?

Generally, a hotter area has better blood flow. Massage promotes good blood flow and results in an increase in temperature on the skin surface. However, if one area is very hot and your cat shows reluctance to have you massage there—conveyed by having her ears drawn back, whiskers bristled and forward, eyes wide, and/or a twitchy tail—she may have an injury. Skip the massage in that spot until another day.

Because cooler areas tend to indicate that blood circulation is slow, muscles in that spot may be tense and sore. Your cat will probably show that she welcomes a massage by purring loudly, putting her ears forward, half-closing her eyes, or by pushing her body into your hands.

Texture and tension are two more qualities you can feel during *effleurage*. They are difficult to describe accurately, so give yourself an idea of what a tense muscle feels like by doing this quick exercise:

• Rest your left forearm on a desk or the arm of a chair, palm down. Gently press on the muscles of your forearm with the fingers of your right hand. The muscles should feel soft and relaxed.
• Now clench your left hand into a fist and feel the muscles again. The muscles are now tense and feel harder and tighter.

Older cats will generally feel more tired and stiff than younger cats. Tensions have built up from years of hunting, marking territories, and producing kittens. Always take note of the tension in your cat's body as you use these familiar strokes.

Putting together the information gained through *effleurage* lets you assess your cat's needs before you go on to deeper massage strokes.

*That feels lovely! Your cat may express her appreciation of your massage technique by pressing her body into your hands.*

# Tapping

**This is a gentle tapping done only on the bigger muscles. It stimulates the nervous system and promotes circulation in the muscles at a deeper level than palming strokes. It helps release muscle tension by stimulating blood flow to the area and warming the muscles by creating mini-contractions.**

This is also called *petrissage*. Use your fingers in a slow 1, 2, 1, 2, 1, 2 rhythm Start very gently. If you start heavily, you could bruise your cat instead of soothing her muscles. She may then run from you with her ears back, twitching her tail fiercely.

As you and your cat feel more confident, speed up. If she stretches into your hands, she is asking you to increase the pressure slightly.

It is important to use *petrissage* only on larger muscles—on the lower part of the shoulders but not over the shoulder blades, and very gently along the back, and through the hindquarters.

Be very careful: If you do this stroke in places where her bones are close to the surface, you can cause bruising, so avoid these areas.

*A happy cat will purr in time to the rhythm of your tapping fingers. Once you've learned to do this stroke properly, it will feel wonderful, and your cat will show her total approval.*

# compression

**This stroke achieves a level of stimulation similar to or deeper than tapping. Compression is commonly used after tapping, because it releases muscle tension and promotes deep relaxation. Compression strokes are similar to palming but are short and deep rather than gentle and sweeping. A circular motion works very well.**

Apply only light pressure on those areas where the skin lies close to the bone, such as the top of the neck, the shoulder blades, and the tops of the hind end and legs. Keep checking for differences in temperature, texture, and tension, and keep a tab on her responses.

# sweating

The "sweating" stroke is sometimes used during compression. If you find an area that is particularly cool, pause with your hand cupped or laid gently on that spot for a minute or two. This allows heat to build up under your hand and gets the blood circulating to promote relaxation. If your cat is sensitive in one spot, sweating gives her time to relax before you start massaging again. This is particularly important if she is normally nervous and needs a lot of reassurance before trying something new.

When you have completed the compression strokes, your cat should be very relaxed and comfortable. The aches and pains of stiff muscles will have eased away. She may be sleepy. Do a few more strokes to signal that the massage is over, using either light compression or palming.

*Compression is a very useful stroke to learn, as it relieves knots of muscle tension and makes your cat wonderfully relaxed and contented.*

# 4

## a head-to-tail massage

# the right time and place

Choose a time that suits you both. It could be at night or a quiet time in the morning, as long as you and your cat are feeling mellow and in the right mood to give and receive. Start off with weekly massage sessions and gradually make it part of your daily routine. Think how much better a massage feels in gentle, pleasing surroundings. Soft lighting, relaxing music, and time away from telephones or televisions will enhance the treatment. Your cat will appreciate a calm, soothing ambience and will be more receptive to your touch.

# a safe pair of hands

Wash your hands before starting and again after you finish. Although they are fastidious about keeping clean, there is generally a touch of dirt or oil on any fit and active cat.

To ensure that the massage is comfortable for your cat, your fingernails should be shorter than the ends of your fingertips. If your nails are long, jagged, or sharp, trim them so they don't stab your cat. Otherwise, be *extremely* careful! You can adapt the sequence below so that you can do it with long nails. Where you are instructed to use your fingertips, you should use the pads of your fingers instead.

If your cat is lying on her tummy, the first sequence is performed simultaneously on both sides of her body. If she prefers to lie on her side, massage first one side, then the other.

# get yourself relaxed

**Your cat will only enjoy a massage if you are completely relaxed. She will sense your tension if you've had a bad day, so it may be better to postpone it for another time. Also, allow plenty of time for the session.**

A tense, rushed massage will make your cat feel apprehensive rather than soothed. In fact, she is likely to make a quick exit the next time you try to massage her.

**Before starting, spend some time relaxing yourself. Here are some techniques to try:**

**1** Find a comfortable chair. Have a glass of water or your favorite non-alcoholic drink. Clear your mind of the day's hassles.

**2** Next, imagine your toes becoming heavy and relaxed. Then imagine the same for your feet. Send this sensation up your legs to your knees, to your rear. Start again with your fingers and move the "heavy" sensation through your hands to your elbows, to your shoulders. Apart from the gentle movement as you breathe in and out, your whole upper body should be relaxed and quiet. Shake your hands gently, letting your fingers flop.

**3** Now stand up. Move calmly and quietly toward your cat, talking to her gently to reassure her.

## Step 1
### long body strokes

Approach your cat with your hand out. If she sniffs it and rubs against it, take that as confirmation of her willingness to have a massage.

Start by using palming strokes. Run your hands down her body, one after the other, simply stroking her. Then cup your hands over her body and exert a very light pressure with your palms and fingers. Gradually increase the pressure until she is pushing back into your hands. Don't press any harder or she may decide that massage is not for her.

Work from behind the ears at the top of the neck, down the neck, and to the end of the hindquarters in long, slow movements. Look for signs that she is enjoying the attention. Loud purring, closed eyes, and ears pricked forward indicate a truly happy cat.

*A loving hand held out to your cat promises her a delightful massage session. If she rubs her cheek against your hand, then she's happy to proceed.*

If your cat's ears flick backward, it may mean that the area is sensitive. Be very gentle—if you suspect an injury somewhere or other contraindications are present, avoid that spot until the area has healed.

## Step 2
## down to the paws

You can massage the paws as a continuation of each leg, with the cat sitting or lying down. If she is sitting upright, slide your hands from her shoulders and down her forelimbs to her paws. Cup your fingers around her limbs for an all-around limb massage. Flatten your fingers to stroke the top surface if she is lying down.

Some cats are very sensitive to having their paws touched. If your cat acts disturbed or pulls away, respect her feelings and leave her paws alone. After she is more familiar with massage, you can draw her into becoming fully accustomed to having her paws touched.

*Before you reach your cat's paws, let her enjoy your fingers enclosing and stroking her legs in a gentle, flowing motion. This will prepare her for being touched on her paws.*

If she is enjoying the strokes on her forelimbs, you can repeat these several times before proceeding to the next stage.

Follow the same routine down her hind limbs, always using a light pressure. Slide your hands gently along her back to her hindquarters, then down to her paws.

As with her front legs, cup your fingers and use a light pressure for an all-around limb massage. If your cat is lying on her tummy, just stroke the top surface of her limbs.

## Step 3
### stroking the tail

Your cat will often encourage you to stroke her tail when she's winding her body around your legs, so she should really enjoy a focused tail massage like this. Use *effleurage* strokes along her tail, gently enclosing it with your palm and fingers, and using long, continuous movements. Her tail is very sensitive, so be careful never to pull or twist it. Apply a very light pressure initially and gradually increase it until she presses her tail upward into your hands or keeps it very relaxed.

Watch out for those tell tale pleasure signals: yawning, gently curving her tail, and purring.

*Tail up and pressing into your hand—your cat gets ecstatic pleasure from having her tail massaged with gentle effleurage strokes.*

## Step 4
## shoulder drumming

Up until this point, you have been using soothing, relaxing palming strokes. Now you can introduce tapping or *petrissage* to stimulate your cat's muscles, circulation, and nervous system.

Practice drumming your fingers on your own hand as if you were bored or fed up. You are going to use this motion on your cat's muscles.

Search just behind the bony shoulder blades for the softer-feeling shoulder muscles. Relax your fingers, then drum them on the muscles very gently and slowly. Avoid tension in your fingers; tight fingers will land heavily and may cause bruising. Relaxed fingers will bounce off her body.

You cat will not have felt anything like this before! Drumming very slowly gives her time to get used to the sensation.

Gradually increase the speed, *not* the pressure, until you are drumming as fast as you can with relaxed fingers.

*Now is the time when you can introduce your cat to something new and healthily stimulating for her system. This is a light drumming stroke—and it's a good idea to try it out on your own hand before using it on your cat.*

*This is a fun stroke to learn. Make your fingers into little running legs—but you should only touch the muscles along either side of the spine.*

Allow your cat to get used to the sensation in each area of the shoulder muscle before moving on to the next spot. Try to keep your speed steady and rhythmical—this will become easier as you become more familiar with massage.

You may not need to move much to cover the whole shoulder if your cat is thin and wiry. The bigger the cat's shoulders, the more you will have to move your hands.

If you find that your hands are growing tense, you should stop and shake them loose for a few seconds. Once your hands feel relaxed, you can resume drumming.

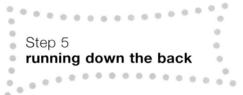

## Step 5
## running down the back

Imagine that your index and middle fingers are a little man's legs— you can practice on the surface of your hand if you want. Lightly run down your cat's back to her hindquarters. Keep your fingers on the muscles on either side of her spine, *not* on her spine. Keep your touch light, relaxed, and steady. Run back up to the shoulders. Repeat this several times.

If she shows signs of tension or worry, do some palming strokes to calm and reassure her. Then return to "running down the back," but be sure to use an extremely light pressure on her.

## Step 6
## hindquarter drumming

Next, you can drum over your cat's hindquarters.
Start slowly with relaxed fingers and a light
pressure. Gradually increase the speed of your
drumming and start moving your hands over the
hindquarter muscles. Drum for several minutes.

These strokes are quite stimulating. Tell your cat
that you are finished with *petrissage* by doing a few
palming strokes to calm and relax her.

## Step 7
## neck Cs

*It's very easy to
make a C shape
with your fore
finger and thumb.
This technique is a
highly effective
way to relieve any
areas of stiffness or
soreness on your
cat's body.*

This is a mild compression stroke. Make a "C"
by curving the first finger and thumb of one hand
toward each other. Place your "C" on the top of the
cat's neck just behind the ears. Press lightly and
rock your hand gently from side to side, moving
from the right to the left side of the neck. Gradually
increase the pressure. Tension is often stored in the
neck, so your cat may soon be pressing back into
your hand with great delight. If she is not pleased

with this attention, you should immediately lighten your pressure. Keep it light until she is more familiar with the feeling.

Slide your hand down her neck and repeat until you are at the base of her neck. You should be able to put a little more pressure on the base of the neck than you can in areas close to her ears.

When your cat has been feeling rather stiff and sore, the back of her neck is one place where she may be feeling most tense. In that case, she should really enjoy the sensation of being massaged in this area. But you should always adapt your pressure to her reactions. Watch her all the time, and monitor her responses closely.

Stay alert to any signals that she wants you to stop the massage. Her tail is a very good indicator. Swished vigorously back and forth, it shows anger. Held up and bristled, it means that she's feeling aggressive and is not willing to be massaged. If she twitches her tail, return to a stroke she likes better or lighten your pressure.

Step 8
**shoulder circles**

Using the tips of your fingers to explore, locate the shoulder muscles behind the bony shoulder blade. Starting with the lightest possible pressure, use the tips of the first and middle fingers of each of your hands to draw tiny circles on these muscles.

Gradually increase your pressure until your fingers sink slightly into the muscles. If your cat is particularly sturdy, you will need to cover more territory than you would if she were tiny.

If your cat enjoys this, she will purr loudly and press into your fingers, or she will have an ears-pricked, eyes-closed look of contentment.

## Step 9
## circling along

You can continue using the same technique to massage further along your cat's body. Place your fingers on the muscles on either side of your cat's spine. You should be able to feel the soft muscles that are located there. Using light pressure, make tiny circles. Gradually move down the spine in small circles, moving slowly and steadily, and *always* lightly, along the muscles.

If your cat wants more pressure, she will arch her back up into your fingers. Allow her to do this rather than increasing the pressure yourself. This way, she can be in control and can dictate the exact amount of pressure she wants.

## Step 10
## hindquarter Cs and circles

This is the final stage of your massage sequence, so your fingers should now return to the "C" position. Place your finger and thumb over the front of your cat's hindquarters. Exerting a light, gentle pressure, rock your hand from side to side. Move your "C" down and continue the side-to-side movements until you reach the top of your cat's hindquarters, just in front of her tail. Repeat once more.

Next, put your hands on your cat's haunches. Using the first and middle fingers of both hands, make tiny circles on the muscles there.

Start with a light pressure and increase it very gradually to a mild pressure. Usually, your cat will enjoy this, but you should watch out for any signs that she is feeling uncomfortable. If her ears flick back or her tail bristles or twitches, return to a lighter pressure or use some "long body strokes" to calm her. Then try again.

To signal to her that the massage is over, and to relax her completely, do a few "long body strokes," "down the paws," and "stroking tails."

At the end of her massage session, she will be very happy and relaxed. It will be a great feeling for you, also, as you will have the satisfaction of consolidating the trust between you and your cat.

*Massage your cat's haunches by making tiny circles with your fingertips. By the time you've arrived at the end of your head-to-tail sequence, she will be in feline heaven—relaxed, happy, and purring with pleasure.*

# 5 stately age, frisky youth

# elderly cats

**Massage is extremely beneficial for older cats, especially those suffering from chronic ailments such as arthritis. It eases sore, tired muscles and aching joints by increasing the blood circulation and supply of oxygen to them. However, you should always check for symptoms that indicate your cat should not be massaged. If you are in any doubt about her health, consult your vet before beginning.**

This massage sequence is specially designed to be lighter in impact for senior citizen cats because they are less robust than youngsters. It incorporates more gentle *effleurage* and light compressions than the usual vigorous percussion strokes.

Before starting, increase your cat's overall comfort by adding extra warmth to her bedding. This is particularly welcome on cold or damp days, when older cats tend to feel stiff. It is not necessary on hot days or if you are massaging in a sunny spot.

You can use microwavable heat packs to warm her bed. Heat the packs on "high" for two minutes and place them under her blanket. In a few minutes, the warmth will start to filter through to her body. Alternatively, you can place her blanket on a warm radiator to heat, or use a partially-full hot water bottle. If you use a hot water bottle, wrap it up well so that your cat doesn't pierce it with her claws.

If your cat is on her tummy during this sequence, massage both sides of her body at the same time. However, you'll find that older cats often favor one side. If this is the case, massage one side first, then gently turn her over and massage the other.

*When your cat becomes a senior citizen, she'll certainly
appreciate extra warmth and comfort in her bedding.
Try microwavable heat packs—she'll feel blissfully cozy.*

## softly, softly, body strokes

With an open hand, and using a light palming stroke, start at the top of the cat's neck, behind the ears. Begin by doing this as gently and lightly as possible. Continue down the neck and back, using long, slow movements of one hand after the other, moving all the way along to the end of her hindquarters.

Gently increase the pressure until your cat is purring and her eyes are half-closed.

Older cats are highly sensitive. Watch for signs she uses to tell you if she is uncomfortable. If her ears are flicking backward, her whiskers bristling forward, or she is growling, be gentle or skip that spot.

Step 2
## fingertipping the paws

Starting with the forelimbs, use the tips or pads of your first two fingers to make short, gentle strokes of about 1 inch (2.5cm) or so on the front and side of each of your cat's legs. Work your way down her forelegs toward her paws. Use a light touch, but make sure that you don't tickle her!

Work your way down her forelegs again, using slightly firmer strokes. You need to make these strokes far more delicate on your older cat than the long sweeps with cupped hands you use for youngsters.

Older cats tend to be stiff and many of them have arthritis in some joints. If your cat looks uncomfortable or moves her paws away, stop "fingertipping" before you reach her paws.

If your cat enjoys having her forelimbs and paws massaged with this "fingertipping" stroke, you can go on to a gentle "down to the paws," as described on page 57. Be very careful not to use a twisting motion, though, which could strain her legs.

Repeat all of these steps on her hind legs.

## Step 3
## stroking the tail

Your elderly cat will adore having her tail gently stroked like this. Enclose her tail with your palm and fingers. Apply very light pressure so that you can only just feel her tail, but do not pull or twist it, as that would be very uncomfortable for her.

Watch her reaction. She will press her tail upward into your hands or keep it very relaxed to indicate pleasure. This is the same stroke you use on a younger cat, except a lighter pressure is applied.

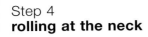

## Step 4
## **rolling at the neck**

"Rolling" is an excellent technique to use on an older cat, and is much more relaxing for her than percussion strokes. Find the area at the top of the neck, where a mother cat would pick up her kittens. Now pick up a tiny amount of skin—just enough to hold—between your thumbs and first fingers.

The rest of her skin will stretch out as you hold onto the roll. Gently roll the skin back and forth between your fingers, then release it. Use "rolling" at the sides of her neck as well. But don't try it under her neck. This is your cat's throat and she will not appreciate it!

If your cat is healthy, the skin should recoil fairly quickly. If it doesn't, she may be dehydrated. In this case, stop your massage immediately and consult the vet.

*That feels wonderful! Your elderly cat will appreciate this relaxing stroke, and it's a great way of gently stimulating her system.*

## Step 5
## rolling along the body

Now work gently down her back, shoulders, and haunches—
anywhere you can find enough skin to pick up. Needless to say, her
limbs, tail, head, and throat are not suitable areas for this stroke.

If your cat shows any sign of discomfort with this procedure, return
to "softly, softly, body strokes" and after she is relaxed, try again
using a much lighter touch.

## Step 6
## neck Cs

As for a younger cat, massage her neck by making a "C" shape
with the first finger and thumb of one hand. Now place it over her
neck, just behind the ears. Lightly, gently, rock your hand from side
to side to produce a mild compression stroke.

Your old cat may enjoy this so much that she presses her body up
and into your hand. In this case, you can increase the pressure very
slightly. Keep monitoring her responses as you work, however, and
always err on the side of caution.

## Step 7
### back Cs

Using the "C," start from your cat's shoulders and gradually progress all the way down her back to her haunches. Use a light, even pressure. Let your cat tell you how much pressure she wants by stretching her back up into your hands. Don't increase your pressure on her back— you may cause her discomfort rather than pleasure, especially if she has a prominent spine and ribs.

## Step 8
### hindquarter Cs

At the base of the tail and using very light pressure, repeat this stroke several times over her hindquarters.

At this point, you should finish off with a brief sequence of strokes that will clearly indicate to your cat that the massage is over. For this purpose, always use a few "softly, softly, body strokes" and "stroking tails." By ending every massage session with this invigorating burst of stimulation to the blood supply in her muscles, you will relax your cat and fill her with contentment. She will probably want to lie down in a quiet spot and enjoy a rest.

# massaging a kitten

Kittens are so adorable that it's easy to spend most of your time cuddling and playing with them. Massage is an excellent way to begin a firm friendship while also teaching your little ball of fluff to accept gentle touches anywhere. This will help immensely when you need to take her to the vet and also helps to make her a sociable cat that doesn't reject your human visitors.

# gently does it!

A kitten massage must be very gentle. Use only your fingertips and the lightest possible pressure. Monitor her responses as you do with older cats. Purring, meowing, eyes closed, yawning, and ears pricked forward are signs that she is enjoying herself.

Your kitten wants to stop if her ears are held to the sides or backward, if her pupils are like deep pools, or if she squirms to get away.

Kittens have so many things to look at, listen to, smell, taste, and touch that they have a hard time being still for any length of time—except to sleep. Don't be upset if she would rather investigate a new arrival, a patch of sunshine, or a leaf blowing than lie still for a massage. When she comes back to see you, just continue with light strokes.

● *Your kitten is usually so busy playing that you will have to catch her first before beginning her massage session.*

## Step 1
### fingertip body strokes

Once you have your kitten settled happily in your lap, very lightly slide the fingers of both hands over her body, from the back of her head to her neck, along her back, and down to the tip of her tail. If necessary, and if she is amenable to this, you can use one hand to keep her quiet and steady while you massage with the other.

## Step 2
### first fingertip face rub

This stroke needs considerable care, but it's important to do it confidently and well, as it gets your kitten accustomed to having your fingers near her eyes and whiskers.

Using an index finger, very gently rub your kitten's face—the top of her head, her cheeks, and under her chin, following the lay of the fur. You must always be very careful to avoid her eyes and the inside of her ears. Your patience will be rewarded in time. She may only tolerate a few rubs at first, but soon she will get used to this and will enjoy many more.

*A delicate touch with your fingertip is all it takes to gently introduce your kitten to the new experience of having her face massaged. She will find this game highly entertaining!*

You are teaching your kitten in a relaxed and non-confrontational way to accept your touch on her face and head. This will make it so much easier when you want to check the condition of her teeth and gums, put a worming tablet inside her mouth, or apply any medication. The vet will thank you!

## Step 3
### handling her paws

Just as you will reap great benefits from teaching your kitten to enjoy having her head touched, you'll also reap the advantages of teaching her to enjoy it when someone handles her legs and paws. A relaxed, unafraid kitten is far less likely to lash out with her claws, and will accept visits to the vet with aplomb.

For this step, use a fingertip to stroke slowly and gently down a limb to the paw. Your kitten may think this is a wonderful game—watch out for those needle-sharp, tiny claws!

If she reaches for you with her claws out, stop. Wait until she has forgotten about the game and then stroke down the leg to the paw again.

Once your kitten shows you that she enjoys the fingertip strokes down her legs and over her paws, gently hold the whole limb in one hand and slowly stroke it with the other hand.

*Loving and trusting, your kitten will learn to hold out her paw so that you can massage it lightly with a fingertip.*

## Step 4
## finger-tickling tummies

An adult cat displays her tummy for two reasons. The first is to indicate submission to a larger and more aggressive cat, and the second is to express pleasure—she will roll over on her back when she basks in a warm, sunny spot, for example. The belly is a very sensitive area. Many cats react to a touch on this area by curling into a ball or by unsheathing their claws.

It's important to help your kitten to overcome her reservation about letting someone touch her underside. Tickle her tummy very lightly with the first and middle fingertips of one hand. Start by tickling for only a few seconds until she gets used to the feeling.

*It's great fun to tickle a kitten's tummy, as it instills trust between you both. But you must be careful. If you're a little rough and go too far, she'll catch your finger with her needle-sharp claws.*

## Step 5
## fingertip circles

Using one finger on a small kitten—two fingers on a larger one—make tiny circles starting on the top and sides of your kitten's neck. Avoid her throat. Move down her body, making circles all the time. Be aware of the tendency for the circles to increase in size and remember that you should always keep them tiny.

*Gentleness is extremely important!* A kitten is so delicate that you will probably be able to feel her bones. If you use too much pressure, you'll bruise her or worse. Use an extremely light touch.

## Step 6
## back to the body strokes

It is most important to reassure your kitten whenever she needs it—this is a completely new experience for her. You are not conforming to a rigid schedule, so give her time. You want her to think of massage as wonderful and relaxing. If she is wary and disconcerted by her new experiences, be patient and return to "fingertip body strokes," which mimic a mother cat licking her kitten. If she curls up or grabs your hand with her claws, she's decided to have a rollicking game, probably because she has become distracted. So stop. Repeat some more "fingertip body strokes." Then try again. As she gets used to this sensation, build up the time you work second by second. Eventually, she will be happy to be massaged for minutes at a time. After she settles down, try moving on to the next step.

## Step 7
## tippy tails

If your kitten has been able to concentrate for this long, you should complete her massage by getting her used to having her tail touched. You do this by using your fingertips to make long, light strokes from the base to the tip of her tail. Then make shorter strokes of only 1 inch (2.5cm) or so and work slowly down the tail. Return to the longer fingertip sweeps.

Don't try to hold her tail just yet. Save this for when she grows up. Never pull or twist her tail, as that would frighten her.

When you have finished the massage, allow your kitten a few minutes to relax and doze on your lap. She needs time to absorb what you have done and to enjoy the pleasurable sensations post-massage. Your happy, contented kitten will want to be massaged time and time again.

# and finally, a nice rest

After her massage, allow your cat to rest quietly. She may want to drink more than usual, so give her some fresh water. Drinking helps flush out the toxins that the massage has released. Make sure that she can get outside or that her litter box is clean. She will probably need to relieve herself once or twice more than usual.

A warm, comfortable bed will help her to get the most from a massage (see page 72). An older cat may appreciate two warmed blankets—one to lie on while being massaged and the other to rest on after the massage is over and the first blanket has cooled down. You could try a warmed blanket on top of an older cat, although some won't like it.

Don't feed your cat for at least half an hour after a massage. Digestion draws the blood to the stomach and intestines, but your cat needs a high level of circulation in her muscles and joints until the toxins have been expelled.

Every cat is an individual. After the massage and over the next few hours, observe what she does and where she goes. Generally, the best ideas about what your cat enjoys come from her! She is usually very good at telling you what she wants.

# other touch therapies

## Acupuncture

A traditional Chinese treatment, veterinary acupuncture dates back over 3,000 years. It is based on the theory that an animal has a healthy circulation of life force, or *qi*, that flows along well-defined channels known as meridian or energy lines. The *qi* keeps the body in perfect balance and health. Acupuncturists insert very fine needles at points along the meridians to stimulate or suppress energy.

These meridians are connected to the internal organs, muscular and joint structures, and the nervous system. Acupuncture points are places on these meridians where the flow of *qi* can be influenced. In animals that are unwell, the flow of *qi* energy becomes disturbed. In this case, the acupuncturist will manipulate energy flow by stimulating the acupuncture points, and thereby rectify certain disorders.

Animal therapists mostly use acupuncture to enhance healing, and will treat cats for pain-related problems such as arthritis, tendon injuries, and back pain. The most enthusiastic proponents claim that an even wider range of cat illnesses responds well to acupuncture.

These include problems like arthritic disorders or muscular injuries, inflammation of the liver, gynaecological problems in female cats, and reproductive disorders in male cats. Acupuncture is also said to help cats who are suffering from hormonal disorders, including pituitary, thyroid, parathyroid and adrenal dysfunctions. It can also be used to regulate blood sugar levels by stimulating insulin production.

## Acupressure

Acupressure works in the same way as acupuncture but, instead of needles, the therapist uses his or her fingers to apply a steady pressure (*tuina*) to acupressure points. The Japanese developed a similar form of massage, known as *anma*.

## Shiatsu

Based on the same principles as acupuncture and acupressure, this technique was introduced to Japan over 1,500 years ago. Cat and dog shiatsu is practiced widely there, and also in Australia. Literally meaning "finger pressure," the treatment covers the entire body, stimulating muscle relaxation and circulation.

## Trigger point therapy

Originating in China, but adapted by Western conventional medical teaching, this technique treats muscle pain. Pain is not always felt at the site of the injury; frequently, it is experienced at a referred point. The therapist applies firm pressure to these points, which may result in initial discomfort, but is followed by release and pain relief. The response to Trigger Point Therapy is fast for recent problems and a little longer for chronic pain.

## TTouch therapy

Developed by Canadian horse trainer Linda Tellington-Jones TTouch is a gentle therapy that works only at skin level. Using relaxed fingers, you make circular movements, and tailor them to each particular cat. The method is used to calm nervous cats and helps with training by relaxing them and focusing their attention.

# index

Published by MQ Publications Limited

12 The Ivories, 6–8 Northampton Street

London N1 2HY

Tel: +44 (0) 20 7359 2244

Fax:+44 (0) 20 7359 1616

email: mail@mqpublications.com

website: www.mqpublications.com

Copyright © MQ Publications Limited 2004

Text © 2004 Nicola Routledge

Illustrations © 2004 Bo Lundberg

Editor: Yvonne Deutch

Design: Lindsey Johns

ISBN: 1-84072-598-2

10 9 8 7 6 5 4 3 2 1

Printed and bound in China

This book contains the opinions and ideas of the author. It is intended to provide helpful and informative material on the subjects addressed in this book and is sold with the understanding that the author and publisher are not engaged in rendering medical, health, or any other kind of personal professional services in this book. The reader should consult his or her medical, health, or competent professional before adopting any of the suggestions in this book or drawing references from it. The author and publisher disclaim all responsibility for any liability, loss, or risk, personal or otherwise, which is incurred as a consequence, directly or indirectly, of the use and application of any of the contents of this book.